SMALL-GROUP
READING INSTRUCTION

by Adria F. Klein
Barbara Andrews
Peter Afflerbach

Welcome to PD Essentials!

What is essential in teaching and learning? This is a huge question
for educators and one we try to answer in this series of professional
books. This PD Essentials Comprehensive Literacy Series by Benchmark
Education is for both experienced and new teachers. Whether the
discussion involves thinking through new ideas, reinforcing and
strengthening best instructional practices, or adding tools for doing
assessment that informs instruction, we have written these books from
a practitioner's point of view.

For this book, *Small-Group Reading Instruction*, we thought about the
key questions teachers might have when working with small groups.
Certainly, we needed to address the best practices of guided reading,
strategic groups, and close reading—and how to implement those
successfully in the classroom and monitor progress. Targeted support
for English Learners and suggestions for differentiation for special
learning needs are provided. There are suggestions in the book for
further reading as well as key references from reading research. One
other helpful component in each book is a glossary of relevant terms,
so that teams can discuss and develop a shared common language for
collaboration.

Adria Klein, Ph.D., Series Author

Table of Contents

PUTTING IT IN PERSPECTIVE

How can we manage independent work time as we meet with small groups of students?

What is the role of small-group reading in a comprehensive literacy framework?

What are the roles of students and teacher in different approaches to small-group reading instruction?

What opportunities exist to incorporate different types of small-group practices?

Small-group reading instruction is a part of almost every reading program—and for good reason. Effective instruction is personal and intensive, and instructing students in small groups allows us to provide them with this personalized and intensive instruction. Using appropriately selected books, we can target our instruction and provide feedback to each group member, so that all students get precisely the support they need to make progress.

Small-group reading instruction is also an essential component of a comprehensive literacy framework. A key feature of comprehensive literacy is that it is based on the gradual release of responsibility approach to teaching and learning. The gradual release of responsibility was developed by literacy researchers P. David Pearson and Margaret Gallagher (1983) from the work of psychologist Lev

Vygotsky. It suggests that adults should teach and support students at "the growing edge of the [their] competence" (Bruner, 1986). In a gradual release approach to teaching a strategy, students first observe the teacher, who is modeling how and when to use the strategy, and is responsible for this aspect of the lesson (*I do*). Then students observe and participate in small intervals of practice (*I do, you help*). Next, students take on more of the work, practicing the new learning while we provide support (*you do, I help*). Then, students apply the strategy on their own (*you do, I watch*) while still in the classroom, so we can observe and return scaffolding if it is clearly needed. Finally, students begin to transfer their learning to independence. Students adjust, apply, and adapt the strategies by taking full responsibility of their learning. Small-group reading instruction is generally the *you do/I help*, or practice, part of the gradual release model. The teacher guides students, but students are doing more of the work.

> 66
> While small-group work is at the heart of guided reading, it must not be seen as an end in itself . . . Small-group guided reading, as powerful as it is, must be understood as but one part of a comprehensive literacy program.
> *Regie Routman, 2002*
> 99

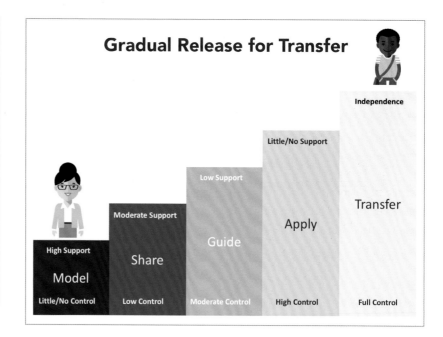

Why do we advocate for small groups? There are several compelling answers: to prepare students to be independent, to apply and practice strategies they have been learning, and for them to do it on their own in an environment of support in school. This leads to a stronger sense of self, contributes to the development of student agency and identity, and creates skillful student decision makers as their understanding and reasoning is applied in new learning situations.

Why and How to Assess

The HOW of three types of small-group instruction is the major focus of this book. These three types are described in the chart on page 10. Assessment information is also included. How do we determine a student's level of learning so that we can best scaffold our instruction? Teachers need detailed assessment information when placing students in small-group reading instruction. Our goal here is to determine, with confidence, each student's zone of proximal development. This helps us meet each student at the current point of potential growth. In general, the more assessment information we have for students as it relates to the small-group goals, the more accurate our placement of students in those groups and the more responsive our instruction will be. Assessments such as reading inventories provide detailed information about students' achievement, including fluency, sight words, and approximate reading comprehension levels.

As well, our amassed understanding of each student is helpful. What have we learned since the school year began about students' reading? Their answers to comprehension questions, the degree of fluency with which they read, their speaking and writing vocabularies—each of these information sources helps us identify the zone of proximal development.

Assessment to Inform Instruction
What are the most efficient means of formative assessment?

Identifying students' zones of proximal development is a key to small-group reading success. Fortunately, we have an array of assessments with which we can regularly determine these zones. We can use our overall understanding of students to determine their instructional level. Just as we construct meaning when we read a book, teachers construct meaning of students, by using formative assessment information. This construction of meaning fuels our accurate determination of student strengths and needs—it helps us accurately identify the zones of proximal development. Our experiences with listening to students read, asking them comprehension questions, and requesting retellings all focus on formative assessment. Joining the incoming stream of formative assessment information with what we already know about our students offers the best opportunity to identify zones of proximal development, and to have successful teaching and learning.

Starting with the WHY

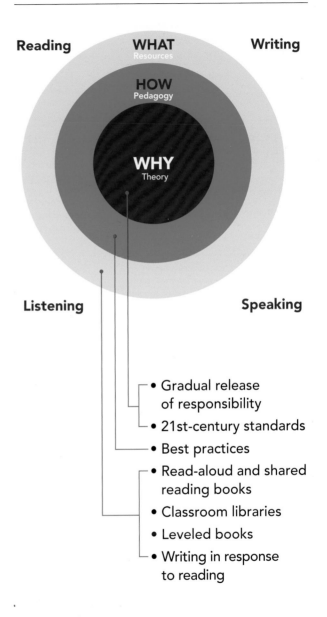

Reading   WHAT
Resources   Writing

HOW
Pedagogy

WHY
Theory

Listening   Speaking

- Gradual release of responsibility
- 21st-century standards
- Best practices
- Read-aloud and shared reading books
- Classroom libraries
- Leveled books
- Writing in response to reading

Types of Small-Group Reading Instruction

	GUIDED READING	STRATEGY GROUPS	CLOSE READING
Text Level	Instructional Level	May be at or below instructional level	Instructional level or higher
Basis for Forming Groups	Students at the same or similar reading levels	Students struggling with the same strategy who may be at different reading levels	Students at the same or similar reading levels with some variety possible, depending on specific student learning goals
Types of Text Used	Unfamiliar, usually short informational or fiction texts selected by the teacher. All students read the same text. Teacher generally selects text but can give students some limited choices.	Often are familiar books to facilitate specific strategy use. Students may focus on same strategy use but use different books. Teacher or student may select text depending on purpose. Text may need to be genre specific.	Shorter texts or parts of texts of all genres that warrant closer attention. Usually read and reread for deeper understanding
How Text Is Read	Teacher provides an introduction and states the purpose for reading. Students read the text to themselves, or aloud quietly, at the same time. The teacher may ask certain students to whisper-read, to enable the teacher to listen in and prompt or scaffold if necessary.	Students read the text or texts silently or aloud quietly and simultaneously, while the teacher observes and prompts them to use a specific strategy. Connects to and amplifies classroom instruction.	The first reading, especially in Kindergarten and Grade 1, can be a shared read. Students then reread a text analytically—often annotating as they read—looking at how the text is organized, at an author's vocabulary choices, at the text's key arguments and inferential meanings, and at the author's purpose. The goal is deeper understanding.
How Text Is Discussed	The teacher guides and scaffolds the book discussion with the goal of ensuring that students both comprehend the text and understand the lesson's focus reading strategy. This enables them to transfer strategies and skills to their independent readings.	Teacher-supported discussion of the reading strategy, and how it can be applied to all the texts students are reading as part of the group and independently Again, the goal is to transfer to independent reading work.	Students discuss the text, focusing on the purpose of the close reading lesson. Open-ended questions are asked, and answers are supported with text evidence. Evidence may be verbatim or paraphrased.
Assessment	Teachers' questions focus on text comprehension. Students may also retell. Teachers observe and listen to any student reading aloud—to help determine the nature and success of students' strategy use.	Teachers' questions focus on text comprehension. Students may also retell. Teachers observe and listen as students use their reading strategies. Teachers may also ask students about their strategy use.	Teachers' questions may focus on higher order thinking—as this is often required of close reading. Teachers also use comprehension questions and student retellings. Teachers listen to students in classroom discussion for further information about comprehension and strategy use.

Formative assessment for determining strategy group membership should focus on student reading comprehension. Prior to small-group strategy instruction, teachers should determine what strategies students can use, and what strategies are challenging. This process is straightforward. If we ask a series of literal comprehension questions, and the student answers each successfully, we may infer that the strategies related to literal comprehension are working well. In contrast, consider when the questions we ask require students to use prediction strategies, or summarization strategies. If the students' responses to our questions are not correct, we may infer that they need more work with such strategies. Finally, we can ask students about the strategies they use as they read. We can ask students to think aloud as they use reading strategies, and this can give us a fairly rich portrait of their current reading strategy repertoire.

When grouping for close reading, we can use an approach like that for strategy grouping. Close reading represents an amalgam of reading strategies, so determining what close reading strategies to teach can also be done in a manner such as that used in strategy groups. As in strategy grouping, we can identify students for particular close reading small groups by examining their responses to our questions. Should student responses to these questions consistently fall short, we can infer that we have identified an appropriate zone of proximal development.

What are indicators that students are progressing successfully through a lesson?

We can use assessment mind-sets to help us gauge student progress through a lesson. When we observe, we should be on the lookout for obvious signs of success, or trouble. When students in our small groups become frustrated, or when a conversational student becomes silent, we may infer that they are encountering difficulty. When students are actively engaged and happy, we may infer that they are meeting with success. When we listen, we should encourage students to give voice to their successes and challenges. This practice not only helps us understand students' progress during a single lesson, it also promotes the development of their metacognition, and aids our comprehension monitoring. Finally, our questions can be directed to find out if comprehension is taking place (e.g., What is the main idea of this paragraph? What was the character's motivation?) or where a reading challenge exists for a particular student (e.g., What part of the text is causing the problem? What strategy might you use here?).

What signs indicate that students are struggling?

As noted above, our observations can indicate that students are encountering difficulties. A student who is visibly frustrated, or a student who is regularly talkative falling silent, are each signs of struggle. Also, the indicators we use in reading inventories—the rate of reading, the accuracy of reading—and periodic comprehension questions will alert us to a student who is struggling.

Teaching for Transfer

Teaching students strategies in different contexts is more likely to result in a transfer of learning. The short, focused lessons used in small-group instruction allow us to closely observe and support students' understanding of strategies, skills, and behaviors that have been taught during whole-group lessons. Here, assessment provides a regular stream of information that we can use to update our understanding of each student and tailor instruction to students' needs. Connecting the learning in this way—having consistent objectives and strategies—promotes deeper learning. And explicitly explaining to students that they should apply the strategies they're practicing as they work independently will further enhance this transfer of learning. When students can transfer their strategic understanding and skills to new or novel text or settings, we are teaching forward for the twenty-first century.

Teaching short, focused lessons of strategies and skills previously taught in whole group promotes deeper learning.

Our goal in writing this book is to provide clear and concise information on effective small-group reading instruction. You'll find chapters on teaching guided reading and strategy lessons with small groups, as well as information on how to teach close reading lessons in small groups. Each type of small-group instruction differs in purpose and planning, as well as in how students should be grouped. We encourage you to examine all types of grouping opportunities in every classroom across all grade levels. These groups are not always distinct, even with different purposes, so we suggest ways to dynamically use the different types of small groups and work flexibly.

Another chapter addresses independent literacy work time— because it is essential that students be able to sustain their learning efforts on their own or with partners while you are meeting with a small group. Management always has to be thought about when incorporating small-group work into your classroom, but the role of small-group instruction in a comprehensive literacy framework is critical. Woven throughout the chapters is assessment information. You'll learn how you can use a range of assessments to make effective instructional decisions for your students that will help them grow as readers and writers.

CHAPTER 1

GUIDED READING

"The whole purpose of guided reading is to help children become independent readers."

Michael P. Ford and Michael F. Opitz, 2011

Guided reading is a highly effective form of small-group instruction during which a teacher observes and listens to each student in turn, using formative assessment to help shape instruction. The main goal of guided reading lessons is to support the transfer of reading strategies so students can apply the learning to their independent reading. In this chapter, you'll learn how to teach guided reading so that all students get the instruction they need to become successful, independent readers.

TOPICS IN THIS CHAPTER

Forming guided reading groups

•

Selecting appropriate texts

•

Planning and delivering effective lessons

For guided reading, select text that supports your instructional goals yet engages your students.

What You Need to Know About Guided Reading

Three key understandings will help you teach effective guided reading lessons. First, you must get to know your students' strengths and needs and determine their instructional reading levels so you can form groups. Second, you need to choose an appropriate text to use with each group—a text that is the appropriate level for the group, supports your instructional goal, and is engaging to students. And, third, you need to be able to deliver lessons that support students in building strategies to help them become independent readers. Assessment plays a key role in all three aspects: getting to know students, choosing appropriate texts, and providing instruction.

Getting to Know Your Students

There are several important ways to get to know your students. At the start of the school year, you can review any information you may have from teachers in the previous grade. Surveys administered within the first few days of school quickly provide information about students' feelings toward reading and their reading interests. Also, you can begin observing students right away, noting things such as their oral language development, vocabulary, fluency, and background knowledge and experience. Look for how students organize their thoughts and materials and how they interact with text and express their thinking about text. Observation, it turns out, is a useful and most available source of assessment information.

On page 17 is part of an anecdotal record sheet that Mr. Martinez, a Grade 4 teacher, created that includes his observations of students. He looked for strengths as well as needs and noted both.

Reading assessment is the next step, using oral reading records to determine students' instructional reading levels. These individually administered assessments allow you to evaluate decoding skills and needs, fluency, and comprehension to determine a student's instructional reading level. Mr. Martinez used screener passages and oral reading assessments to get up-to-date information on students' reading strategies and their reading comprehension. He had students read a brief text (requiring 3–5 minutes), which enabled him to collect information that gave him an approximate sense of where students' achievement levels lay. Confident in the approximation of each student's reading achievement level, Mr. Martinez next conducted an oral reading assessment. Like its relatives the informal reading inventory and running records, this assessment provided information about students' reading processes and products. Mr. Martinez was able to identify students' oral reading patterns, including accurate reading, substitutions, omissions, insertions, repetitions, self-corrections, and use of visual cues. This is process information, and it helped Mr. Martinez assess the manner in which students construct meaning. The oral reading assessment also required students to retell what they had read and to answer comprehension questions. As you might imagine, the administration and interpretation of these assessments demand time and assessment insight. However, the results are well worth the effort, as they lead to accurate identification of texts with which student readers can grow and succeed, and of student strengths and weaknesses to address through instruction.

At right is a list of Mr. Martinez's students and their instructional reading levels based on oral reading assessments. The scale, using letters for instructional reading levels, was developed by Irene Fountas and Gay Su Pinnell (1996). (See page 21 for more information on these levels.) Fountas and Pinnell cautioned educators to understand that the reading level alone does not define a student. Typical of every grade, there is a span of student reading levels in Mr. Martinez's class.

NAME	INSTRUCTIONAL READING LEVEL
Bella	V
Lucy	U
Zach	U
Jordan	U
Grace	U
Anna	T
Diana	T
Erika	S
Patrick	R
Cory	Q
Noel	Q
Stephen	P
Kyle	P
Michael	P
Kimberly	P
Kevin	O
Bryan	O
Keith	O
Aurora	N
Emma	N
Olivia	N
Ian	M
Lily	M
Russell	L
Dale	H
Catherine	G

Mr. Martinez's students' instructional reading levels

Forming Guided Reading Groups

STUDENT Diana DATE 10/5	STUDENT Stephen DATE 10/5	STUDENT Erika DATE 10/6	STUDENT Lily DATE 10/8
•good organizing skills •strong vocab •self-monitoring	•struggles to express thoughts •low vocab •easily distracted	•enjoys reading •struggles to express thoughts in writing	•abandons books •reads word by word
STUDENT Diana DATE 10/12	STUDENT Stephen DATE 10/15	STUDENT Erika DATE 10/12	STUDENT Lily 10/13

Mr. Martinez's observations

Below are the six groups Mr. Martinez established based on students' instructional reading levels as just outlined, and on his observation notes. Students will change groups as they make progress. For example, Mr. Martinez plans to watch Diana closely. He observed that her vocabulary is well developed, and he anticipates that she will progress very quickly.

GROUP 1	GROUP 2	GROUP 3	GROUP 4	GROUP 5	GROUP 6
Michael	Aurora	Kevin	Stephen	Anna	Bella
Catherine	Ian	Bryan	Kyle	Diana	Lucy
	Lily	Emma	Michael	Erika	Zach
	Russell	Olivia	Kimberly	Patrick	Jordan
			Keith	Cory	Grace
				Noel	

Mr. Martinez's preliminary guided reading groups

Mr. Martinez will meet with three groups for twenty minutes each day, so he created the schedule below. Notice that he plans to meet with groups 1 and 2, which have the most challenged readers, more often than with the on-level and above-level groups. All students benefit from some time in small-group work, but not all need the same amount of time, nor do they need to meet so frequently. Students in the challenged groups need extra instructional time and reading practice to be able to "catch up" with their peers.

MONDAY	TUESDAY	WEDNESDAY	THURSDAY	FRIDAY
1	2	1	1	1
2	3	2	3	2
4	5	3	6	4

Mr. Martinez's guided reading schedule by group

Determining Your Instructional Focus

Knowing your students' instructional reading levels and keeping anecdotal notes about their reading behaviors will help you decide on the instructional focus for each of your groups. Of course, comprehension is always a key outcome for students, but the small- group setting allows you to focus on specific instructional goals. For example, one small group may have an immediate need for summarization instruction, while another group may benefit from fluency practice. Instructional focus can be on a range of skills and strategies. For your readers at levels A–C—what is usually termed the emergent reading stage—the focus may be self-monitoring, decoding, concepts about print, or fluency strategies such as cross-checking pictures and meaning or reading with expression. At levels D–M— basically the reading levels from Grade K through Grade 2—you will continue to prompt students to apply self-monitoring and decoding strategies during reading and to develop these skills across a wide variety of text types.

At every level in all text types, it's important to help students build their vocabulary knowledge and comprehension strategies—such as asking and answering questions, summarizing important parts of a text, and analyzing relationships between characters and their actions.

STRATEGIES AND SKILLS: HOW THEY DIFFER

The research evidence is clear: skills and strategies are central to reading success—but the two are different *(Paris, Lipson & Wixson, 1983; Pressley and Afflerbach, 1995).* Additionally, how we think about a skill and a strategy is of the utmost importance—because we cannot possibly teach well those things that we don't carefully define and fully understand.

Reading strategies are deliberate, goal-directed attempts to control and modify the reader's efforts to decode text, understand words, and construct meaning from text. Strategies figure in students' comprehension of text, their determination of the meaning of vocabulary words, and the decoding of words. Control and working toward a goal characterize the strategic reader who selects a specific path to a reading goal (i.e., the means to a desired end). For example, the reader who deliberately pauses after each paragraph to evaluate understanding while reading with the goal of summarizing the text is using strategies. Awareness helps the reader select an intended path, the means to the goal, and the processes used to achieve the goal. The reader can examine the strategy, monitor its effectiveness, and revise the goal or means to the goal (or both), if necessary. If the evaluation of reading at the end of each paragraph signals a lack of understanding, the reader may reread, slow the rate of reading, or consult an authoritative source to determine word meaning. Indeed, the hallmark of strategic readers is the flexibility and adaptability of their actions as they read.

Reading skills are automatic actions that result in decoding and comprehending texts with speed, efficiency, and fluency. They are used out of habit, practiced, and mastered to the point where they function automatically. As such, they are usually deployed much faster than strategies because they do not require the reader's conscious decision-making. This has important, positive consequences for each reader, as all reading work is conducted within the boundaries of our limited working memory systems. That is, the more reading work we can do automatically and without the allocation of memory resources, the more of these resources we have to take on complex reading demands and remember and apply what we learn from reading.

HISTORY OF LEVELING BOOKS

Attempts to level books began long ago. Thorndike's (1921) research on word frequency in English served as the spark for the origination of the readability formula. Many systems followed: Flesch (1948), Fry (1963, 1977), Bormouth (1975), Lexile (1997) and the Accelerated Reader Leveling System (AR) (2001).

Keep in mind that the leveling of books is an inexact science. While there have been many attempts to correlate the various systems, those correlations often show the discrepancies among the different leveling systems. Most of these systems are not effective for the earliest levels because texts are so short and word usage is highly repetitive.
(Afflerbach, Pearson, and Paris, 2008)

Selecting a Book

There are two key factors involved in choosing a book for each of your groups: (1) the level of the text, and (2) the suitability of the text for applying the focus strategy. It is also important to consider students' interest in and familiarity with the topic or story.

There are many different systems for leveling texts. The chart on the next page provides information on three common systems. All designate particular texts at a point on a gradient of difficulty, but do so in different ways. The chart also includes correlations to grade levels and developmental reading levels. It's important to consider aspects of different leveling systems when choosing books for your guided reading groups.

The readability ratings on the chart are approximate, and they do not take into account factors such as students' prior knowledge, nor do they distinguish between genres. For example, a single text may prove daunting for the student who lacks any prior knowledge about the text content, while another student could find the text simple because of relevant prior knowledge. Correlations are limited, but teachers find them helpful as starting points to work across leveling systems.

CONVERSION GUIDE to Benchmark Education's Precise, Consistently Leveled Texts

Developmental Category	Letter Level	Number Level	Grade Level	Lexile® Level Range
Emergent	AA	1	PreK–K	
	A	1		
	B	2		
	C	3, 4		
Emergent/ Early	D	5, 6	K–1	BR*–450L
	E	7, 8		
Early	F	9, 10	1	
	G	11, 12		
	H	13, 14		
	I	15, 16		
Early/ Fluent	J	17, 18	1–2	
	K	20	2	
	L	22, 24		
	M	26, 28	2–3	450L–790L
Fluent	N	30		
	O	32, 34	3	
	P	36, 38		
	Q	40	4	
	R	40, 42		
	S	44	4–5	770L–980L
	T	44, 46	5	
	U	50		
	V	60	5–6	
	W	60	6	
	X	60		955L–1155L
Advanced Fluent	Y	70	6–7	
	Z–Z+	80	8	

*Beginning Reading

SYSTEM	DESCRIPTION
Lexile®	A quantitative measure based on: • syllable count • word count • word length, including repeated long words • sentence length This system is based on a mathematical formula and mainly applies to Grades 2 and up, where there is more text available to measure. It does not specifically distinguish between genres.
Number Levels such as DRA™, Beaver Reading Recovery, and Marie Clay	Qualitative measures based on tests intended to be used for assessments (DRA) and instructional interventions (RR). The levels correlate more closely with the letter system than with the quantifiable/Lexile measures. Both DRA and Reading Recovery have had extensive testing of their measures, but they are not the same system.
Letter Levels Fountas & Pinnell™ Guided Reading Levels	A qualitative measure based on a number of factors depending on reading level. Takes into account: • genre • levels of meaning • text structure • language and literary devices • sentence complexity • vocabulary • knowledge demands placed on the reader • text features • layout and amount of text on a page • age-appropriateness of content This system applies to Kindergarten and up, but has a finer gradient of difficulty below Grade 3. It does not have differentiated criteria for distinguishing between genres.

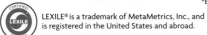

LEXILE® is a trademark of MetaMetrics, Inc., and is registered in the United States and abroad.

Guided Reading Lesson Essentials

- Guided reading groups include six or fewer students at approximately the same instructional level.
- Groups are always flexible and fluid, and students may move to a more appropriate group at any time.
- Lesson texts are always at students' instructional reading level so they provide just a doable amount of challenge.
- Instruction should target specific skills, strategies, and behaviors.
- Assessment information can be gathered through listening to and observing students, as well as through teacher questions and paper-and-pencil assessments.
- Assessment should always guide instruction.
- Most guided reading lessons have three phases: Before Reading, During Reading, and After Reading.

Guided Reading Lesson Structure

No matter what grade level you teach, what your students' reading levels are, or what your teaching purpose is, almost every guided reading lesson will have three phases: Before Reading, During Reading, and After Reading.

BEFORE READING

This part of the lesson should motivate students, make the purpose of the lesson clear, and give students enough information about the text to make it accessible. Here, formative assessment information helps teachers focus on students' most pressing needs—be they cognitive strategies such as decoding abilities, fluency, vocabulary knowledge, comprehension, or full understanding of the purpose of the lesson.

DURING READING

The largest chunk of time in a guided reading lesson is devoted to During Reading (see chart on page 23). This section of the lesson includes students simultaneously reading the text, either whispering or reading very quietly, while you confer with each one individually as needed, providing prompts and support, and taking notes about their progress. Here, your anecdotal observations can be front and center as assessment. You can mark the progress of particular students, while noting challenges for other students. This phase of the lesson takes the most time to learn to do well. The way to learn to do it well is to do a lot of guided reading lessons!

AFTER READING

The After Reading part of the lesson is often brief, but the time we spend on it will vary. Sometimes we will find, as a result of using formative assessment, that more work is needed, that not every student met the goals for the lesson, or that there is variable success across the reading group. When this occurs, we may want to take more time in the After Reading part of the lesson. Don't get locked into one way of planning time in a lesson, but work to meet the needs of the students in that group.

Be sure to successfully wrap up the lesson. Revisit the purpose of the lesson and check students' comprehension by encouraging a discussion about the text and how students used the strategy or skill. This should be a collaborative conversation in which students listen to one another and ask questions. Listen to and document students' responses, making notes about who might need clarification or review of a teaching point. Also, acknowledge students' hard work in applying the strategy.

During Reading:
The teacher listens in, notes reading behaviors, and prompts individual students as needed. Many teachers move next to a student and listen in over the student's shoulder.

PHASES AND TIME FRAME FOR GUIDED READING LESSON

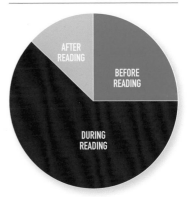

Most guided reading lessons are 15–20 minutes long, and most time is spent on the During Reading part of the lesson.

It's important to point out that Kindergarten guided reading might look different from what is described here, especially at the beginning of the school year. Important initial small-group experiences for Kindergarten students help build community and familiarize students with small-group classroom routines. At times, these lessons may look more like shared reading experiences than guided reading. They give you an opportunity to focus on concepts of print. We need to be acutely attuned to recognize when students are ready to take over some of the reading. For some Kindergartners, this may begin in October, but for others, it may take until the end of the year.

In Action

We are going to visit two classrooms to observe teachers delivering guided reading lessons. As you read, notice how both teachers state the purpose of the lesson and give students plenty of time to have collaborative conversations. Students also will incorporate previously taught strategies as they read. Be sure to notice what they are already controlling and what is on the new edge of their learning. A key to differentiation of instruction is "fresh" and detailed assessment information that teachers gather as the lesson unfolds.

P **Guided Reading Lesson**

Mrs. O'Neal, a Grade 2 teacher, uses an informational text for the purpose of finding key details that support the main topic of the text. This has been the focus of some of her whole-group instruction, including mini-lessons, so students have had opportunities to see her model this strategy. She meets with a group of four students who read at about the same instructional level.

Grade 2 lesson plan before meeting with group

DATE 2/16

TEXT "A Seat on the Bus"   **LEVEL** I/15   Lexile 740L

TEACHING PURPOSE Find Key Details to Support the Main Topic

GROUP MEMBERS Tim, Bill, Adriana, Frank

Before Reading

After distributing a copy of the book to each student, Mrs. O'Neal introduces the book by reading aloud the title and the author's name. Then she shares a brief summary of the book.

> This book tells how people helped change a law that was unfair. It is an informational text. It gives facts and details. What do you think the author of the book wants us to learn? Point to evidence on the cover that supports your answer.

After a brief discussion, she sets a purpose for the day's reading.

As you whisper-read today, pay close attention to key details that support the main topic, fairness. Use your self-stick notes to mark places in the book that have details that help you learn more about fairness.

During Reading

Students begin to whisper-read the book, and Mrs. O'Neal observes, listens in, and briefly coaches each student if needed. She also records anecdotal notes about her students' actions and behaviors. She reinforces the purpose for reading with individual students who may be having trouble focusing. For example, she says:

Remember, we are reading to learn about the topic of fairness. Show me where you placed a note because you found a detail about fairness.

Mrs. O'Neal helps students, as necessary, to decode difficult words in the text, using different prompts depending on what the

During Reading:
Grade 1 students read
the text with support
and prompts from
Mrs. O'Neal.

student's difficulty is. For example, Bill is stuck on the word *judges*. Recognizing that this might be a prior-knowledge challenge, Mrs. O'Neal prompts him to look at the page and think about what word would make sense. She might also prompt for cross-checking text and the illustration, saying:

> Look at the picture and at the beginning letter of the word.
> Can you think of a word that would fit?

Adriana reads "keep" rather than "kept" in a sentence. Mrs. O'Neal knows this is a structural challenge and coaches her, saying:

> You said, "keep." That is close, but the word is *kept*. Read the sentence again using the word *kept*.

After Reading

Mrs. O'Neal guides a group conversation about the book. She reminds students that they know how to look at photographs and captions to find information, a skill they have used many times before. Then she focuses on the purpose of the lesson.

> Who can share what the purpose was today for our reading?

She prompts students to identify the main topic and retell key details in the book. She asks:

What unfair rule did people want to change? Look at page 8. What happened after Rosa Parks would not give up her seat? How did the unfair rule get changed?

Mrs. O'Neal guides students to state their answers based on the main ideas and details in the text, and also to use picture evidence. Where needed to facilitate discussion, she provides sentence frames, such as:

I found a detail. The words say _____. The photograph shows _____. My evidence is _____.

She records the main topic and then on a small tabletop chart adds key details students suggest. If students list a detail that is unimportant, she works with them to support how to distinguish important details from unimportant ones.

She ends the lesson by reminding students to think about key details that support the topic of a text in their independent reading. She adds that there could be details in photos and captions as well as the words.

After Reading: Mrs. O'Neal prompts student discussion.

Readers, remember that thinking about the key details that support the topic of a book will help you understand more of what you read. Some of those details could be in the pictures and captions. Be sure to think about those key details when you read nonfiction books on your own.

Mrs. O'Neal came to the lesson with several goals. The first was to help students learn to find key details that support the main idea. The second was to monitor her students carefully during the lesson so that all available assessment information could be gathered and considered. Mrs. O'Neal's mind-set for assessment is consistent—she views formative, classroom-based assessment as a natural counterpart to instruction.

Mrs. O'Neal depended on two powerful and at-hand general approaches to assessment: observation and listening. Observation of student progress (or of lack of progress) helped alert her to students who were encountering difficulty. With observation, she noticed students who were confident and reading with authority. Contrasting with these students were those who were clearly struggling—they appeared ill at ease in their seats, they lost attention, and they lacked motivation and engagement for the specific reading. Observation was complemented by Mrs. O'Neal's careful listening. She kept an ear out for student questions, for student discussions, and for telltale comments of success or frustration. When listening and observation suggested a teaching and learning opportunity, Mrs. O'Neal was at the ready to take advantage. She used a variety of questions to help students focus on the goal of reading and to remain on task. Digging deeper, Mrs. O'Neal asked questions that helped students identify key details, and then asked questions that helped them connect these key details with the main idea.

I Guiding Reading Lesson

Mr. Roberts, a Grade 3 teacher, has a group of readers who are reading at an instructional level of P/38. He has chosen a biography to focus on summarizing the main idea and key details, which has been the focus of his whole-group lessons. Applying this focus on main idea and key details to multiple text types helps students become more flexible in their use of reading strategies.

DATE 3/27

TEXT Robert Ballard: Deepwater Explorer   **LEVEL** P/38 Lexile 770L

TEACHING PURPOSE Summarizing the Main Idea and Key Details

GROUP MEMBERS Leah, Lucas, Isaac, Hailey

Before Reading

Mr. Roberts opens the lesson.

> This informational text is a biography. Let's think about the
> purpose of a biography.

Before Reading:
Mr. Roberts
introduces biography
to the small group.

Mr. Roberts invites students to flip through the book and view the
illustrations. Then he has students turn to the Table of Contents and
read the titles for Chapters 1–4. He asks how the titles of the chapters
help a reader know this is a biography. Next, he provides information
about the text type and engages students in a conversation to build
more background on it. He then asks students to share what they
already know about the sinking of the *Titanic*.

> What do you think you will learn in this biography of Robert
> Ballard?

After students have spent some time sharing ideas and discussing what they know about biographies and Ballard and the *Titanic*, Mr. Roberts tells them the purpose for the day's reading.

How does the sinking of the *Titanic* figure into this biography? Because we know this story is a biography, when you read, I want you to pay attention to what the main ideas are and the key details that tell about the important events in Ballard's life. As you read the first part of the book, Chapters 1 and 2, look for key words and text features, such as captions and photos, that tell the main idea and key details of Ballard's life. Ask yourself how key details help you learn more in a biography about the life of a person. Use self-stick notes to mark places where you find a key detail.

During Reading

Students begin to read silently or very quietly. Mr. Roberts turns to individual students to ask them to read aloud quietly so he can listen in and coach each student. He takes anecdotal notes as he listens. He observes Lucas making a list of possible key details. He listens to Isaac reason about the relationship between the text and a picture of Ballard's *Argo*. He reminds them of the purpose of the lesson.

During Reading: Mr. Roberts listens to each student read aloud.

Remember, you are looking for key details. Look for key words in the text and in text features, such as captions, that tell you more about Ballard's life. Think about the purpose of key details in a biography.

Mr. Roberts notices that Hailey is struggling.

Hailey, here's what I do to help me think about details. I picture in my mind what I have read. After reading page 7, I picture *Argo* moving slowly at the bottom of the ocean in the deep, dark water. I visualize the scientists sitting on a ship looking at the video screens as they watch *Argo* underwater. Then I use those pictures in my mind to think about the important details on this page.

After Reading

Mr. Roberts supports students in having a collaborative conversation about the main idea and key details in the first two chapters of this biography. Then he tells them they will work together to create a

MAIN IDEA: Robert Ballard, who was always interested in studying the ocean, made important discoveries as a famous oceanographer.

KEY DETAIL: Ballard began studying tidal pools as a child and eventually went to graduate school to study oceanography.

KEY DETAIL: He worked at Woods Hole Oceanographic Institute to help the Navy develop technology to explore the ocean.

KEY DETAIL: Ballard wanted to find the *Titanic*, a luxury ship that sank in 1912.

KEY DETAIL: Ballard used a remotely operated vehicle to search the ocean floor and he found debris that led him to discover the sunken *Titanic*.

Mr. Roberts's chart

summary chart of the key ideas in Ballard's life. After they finish the chart, Mr. Roberts wraps up the lesson. He asks:

> **Why is it important for readers to locate and use key details in a biography?**

Mr. Roberts gives several students time to share with a partner and then with the group.

> **When you continue with your independent reading, think about what details are most important in helping you understand the main idea.**

Mr. Roberts used a combination of formative assessments to teach summarization and key details, and to evaluate student learning. Throughout the lesson, he used several types of questions. One question prompted students to engage relevant prior knowledge. Another question reminded students of their main task. Later in the

After Reading: Mr. Roberts evaluates student learning.

lesson, a further question invited students to reflect on their learning and on the strategies they used to construct meaning. Mr. Roberts made good use of self-stick notes. The notes helped students keep track of their thinking. They were also easily combined to represent the set of key details that support the main idea, and they were an indicator of how well students were doing during the lesson. As he circulated around the group, Mr. Roberts used the self-stick notes in his formative assessment of students' progress and challenges.

Concluding Thoughts

Guided reading lessons are a powerful way to provide students with instruction that focuses on their specific needs. As you listen to your students read, you can prompt and coach them, thoughtfully nudging them toward independence. Supporting students' collaborative conversations at the end of each lesson helps them clarify their thinking, deepen their comprehension, and understand that they should practice further in their own independent reading texts.

Observations and anecdotal notes you make during guided reading help you make decisions about teaching, reforming groups, personalizing your support to students, and deciding on independent reading goals. This information might also help you choose a focus for read-aloud, shared reading, or a mini-lesson.

Reflecting on Your Teaching

Here are some questions to help you reflect on your teaching and to guide professional learning discussions:

- How do you determine when it's time to change membership of your guided reading groups?
- What are some ways you ensure that you are supporting your students' ability to use skills independently after your guided reading lessons?
- What do you find to be the most challenging aspect of guided reading lessons?

FURTHER READING

Next Step Guided Reading in Action, Grades K–2 by Jan Richardson (Scholastic, 2013).

Next Step Guided Reading in Action, Grades 3–6 by Jan Richardson (Scholastic, 2013).

Guided Reading: What's New, and What's Next? by Michael P. Ford (Maupin House, 2015).

Guided Reading, Second Edition: Responsive Teaching Across the Grades by Irene Fountas and Gay Su Pinnell (Heinemann, 2016).

Small-Group Reading Instruction: A Differentiated Model for Beginning and Struggling Readers by Beverly Tyner (International Reading Association, 2009).

Small-Group Reading Instruction: Differentiated Teaching Models for Intermediate Readers by Beverly Tyner (International Reading Association, 2012).

Guided Reading and Literacy Centers by Stanley L. Swartz, Rebecca E. Shook, and Adria F. Klein (Dominie Press, Inc., 2003).

CHAPTER 2

STRATEGY GROUPS

"It made perfect sense that sometimes we should pull a group of students together not because they are reading the same book or reading at the same level, but instead because they would benefit from the same strategy."

Jennifer Serravallo, 2010

Strategy groups are another great tool you can use to accelerate students' reading growth. They allow you to zero in on a very specific strategy with a small group, and provide each student in the group with intensive support. Of course, assessment plays a role in determining which students need what strategies. A guided reading group may have several students who sometimes work together in a strategy group. Both types of groups are needed—and formative, observational assessment will tell you a lot about how to form groups and what is needed. Strategy groups tend to be used more often in Grade 2 and up.

TOPICS IN THIS CHAPTER

Knowing your students so you can form groups

•

Determining the instructional purpose of your lessons

•

Delivering effective three-phase lessons

What You Need to Know About Strategy Groups

Strategy Group Essentials

- As you introduce strategy instruction, make sure students know that the modeling, explanation, and thinking aloud that you provide will be a regular feature of all strategy instruction.
- Membership in strategy groups, like that of guided reading groups, is always fluid and flexible.
- You may meet with strategy groups and guided reading groups both in one day.
- Some students may need to be in more than one group.
- Students should do most of the work, while you support and facilitate the learning.

A strategy group is another teacher-led approach to small-group instruction. The strategy group differs from the guided reading group in several ways. While many strategy groups, similar to guided reading groups, consist of six or fewer students, it is also acceptable to form a larger group of students who need to learn and practice the same skill or strategy. The data you gather from across the literacy day will inform your decisions about group membership and strategy focus. Strategy groups generally meet for shorter periods of time, as their focus is a single comprehension strategy. The group stays together as long as needed to be sure the strategy is understood.

Unlike in guided reading groups, students in strategy groups are likely to be at different instructional reading levels. Because students' levels may vary, students may use different books during the lesson, which the teacher either assigns or has the student self-select. For example, if several students are having difficulty with sequencing and can work with a time line but not understand flashback, the teacher may pick one book for the group to explore, and that book is usually at an easier reading level for most students in the group. Or, the teacher could ask group members to bring a book with a time line, such as a biography, from books they are familiar with from guided reading or their independent reading.

As with guided reading lessons, there should be a through-line of instruction that ensures that a student revisits or learns a skill or strategy in more than one part of the school day. For example, a strategy learned and practiced in the reading strategy group can be used while reading a science article later in the day. This repeated exposure supports teaching for transfer. You can also monitor students to determine whether they are consistently and effectively applying a strategy in their independent work. Here, our close attention to how, when, and why students use their reading strategies provides critical assessment information.

Knowing Your Students and Forming Strategy Groups

How many strategy groups you need will depend on what your formative assessments tell you. These assessments should include observations you made during whole-group instruction, guided reading lessons, and while conferring with students about their independent reading, along with mental notes you have made while listening to students read and use strategies. For example, if you see several students in your class having difficulty using context clues to determine the meaning of a word, it may make sense to establish a group to focus on that. Or you may notice several students able to answer only literal questions and you may decide to have another group focus on making inferences. Some students may meet with guided reading and strategy groups both.

Strategy Group Lesson Structure

A strategy group lesson has a predictable, three-part structure like that of a guided reading lesson, but there are key differences since students are usually reading different books.

BEFORE READING

Before reading, either teach or reteach the strategy, and tell students why using the strategy will help them as readers. This varies by grade level. Clearly state the purpose of the lesson and briefly model application of the strategy, thinking aloud to provide necessary support for students. It is always important to frame students' strategy use in relation to the purpose for reading.

DURING READING

During reading, students practice and apply the targeted strategy as they read their books. Listen to individual students read aloud quietly, coaching them about strategy use as needed while making anecdotal notes. Having a one-minute to two-minute conversation with each student about how the student is applying the strategy to the text will help you provide differentiated scaffolding to each student as needed. Always embed such strategy practice in meaningful tasks.

AFTER READING

After reading, have students review their use of the strategy by discussing examples of places in their text where they applied it. To help students move toward independence, allow them to share their thinking with a partner or the group. Have students discuss their strategy use in relation to their reading goals—which strategies helped them reach what reading goals? Extension activities you might suggest are: continued practice using the same text or a different text; incorporating collaborative conversations about the strategy when students work with partners during independent work time.

In Action

Now let's step inside two classrooms to see how this type of small-group instruction happens in a classroom. As you read, notice how each teacher reviews what the strategy is and quickly reteaches it before the students practice it.

Ⓟ Strategy Group Lesson

In this Grade 2 classroom, Mrs. Evans noticed four students struggling with the strategy of making inferences during whole-group discussions and guided reading lessons. The four students are reading at different levels. She has the students choose texts from their independent reading boxes. She plans to teach the strategy using modeling at the start of the lesson, using a book that all students are familiar with.

Grade 2 lesson plan before meeting with group

DATE 2/10

TEXT FOR STRATEGY MODELING *Panther, Shadow of the Swamp* by Jonathan London, p. 16

STRATEGY FOCUS Making Inferences

GROUP MEMBERS Chloe, Jacob, Caleb, Audrey

Before Reading

Readers, I pulled you together today to talk more about making inferences. Let's review what it means to make an inference. We use this strategy to help us better understand what we read. Making inferences means using information in a text plus our own knowledge to come up with ideas or conclusions about the text.

Here's an example of what I mean. We've read this book before. It's called *Panther, Shadow of the Swamp* by Jonathan

Before Reading:
Mrs. Evans models
the strategy.

London. Let me show you how I made an inference from this book. I read these clues: "She crouches on her belly. Creeps closer and closer. Draws her hind paws beneath her, and extends her claws." I use this description of how Panther is moving, and I connect it with what I know about how cats hunt. I can make a picture in my mind. I have a cat, and this is how my cat looks when she is about to pounce on something. My inference is that Panther is ready to pounce on her prey. I'm going to read another page, and I'd like for you to make an inference from clues in the text. "She spots an armadillo. Good food. But Panther needs more now. Bigger prey." What inference did you make? What were your clues?

She gives them a few minutes to discuss. Students suggest that the words *needs more now* mean that Panther must be very hungry—she would rather hunt for something bigger than an armadillo. Then she reminds them that inferences help us use information from the text and information from our head to make meaning.

While you read your book today, look for clues that help you make inferences. Put a self-stick note beside the clues that helped you infer, so that you can share your clues and the inferences you made when we discuss our use of this strategy.

During Reading:
Mrs. Evans confers
with each student.

During Reading

Mrs. Evans moves around so that she can confer with individual students in the group. Her observations suggest that she needs to reteach the strategy of making inferences. She reminds students that accurate inferences combine information from the text with their prior knowledge. She models making an inference by focusing on a sentence in the text and explaining that she adds something she knows. As students follow her lead, she takes anecdotal notes as she coaches and prompts them.

> I see you've recorded a couple of inferences. How did you come up with those inferences? What clues did you use?

After Reading

Mrs. Evans asks students to think about and share an inference they made in each of their books.

> Think about a place in your book where you made an inference. Turn to your partner and share the inference you made and the clues that support your inference.

Mrs. Evans listens in, observes, and makes anecdotal notes. She uses this formative assessment information to determine that the students have adequately learned and practiced the inference strategy.

> Readers, during your independent reading, continue to think about when you should make an inference and the clues that support your inference. Keep track of the inferences you are making and be ready to describe these inferences to your classmates and me. Remember that making inferences helps you better understand what the author is telling us. This helps us comprehend the book better.

After Reading: Mrs. Evans listens and observes as students share inferences they made in each of their books.

Central to Mrs. Evans's assessment plan was her knowing the content of each of the books that students were reading. While the strategy focus for each student was the same, the book was not. Because the lesson focuses on inferences, Mrs. Evans had to know the content of the different stories so that she could anticipate students' inferences and assist them in making inferences. Mrs. Evans also used modeling, explaining, and thinking aloud to help make the inference strategy tangible for her students. She used direct questions—including "What inference did you make? What were your clues?"—to check on the product of student inferencing. Her questioning revealed that some reteaching was necessary—and this was a key use of her formative assessment.

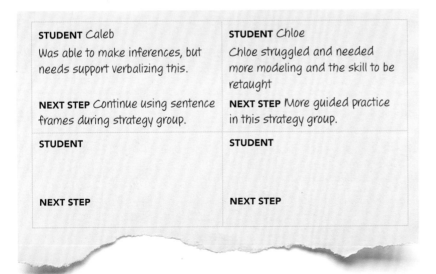

STUDENT Caleb	STUDENT Chloe
Was able to make inferences, but needs support verbalizing this.	Chloe struggled and needed more modeling and the skill to be retaught
NEXT STEP Continue using sentence frames during strategy group.	NEXT STEP More guided practice in this strategy group.
STUDENT	STUDENT
NEXT STEP	NEXT STEP

I Strategy Group Lesson

In this Grade 5 classroom, Mrs. Garza is meeting for the third time with six students who need additional support with using context clues to determine the meaning of domain-specific words in informational text. Mrs. Garza used her observations of individual student work, her careful listening to whole-group discussions, and data from student conferences to determine student membership in this group. Each student has brought to the group today an informational text they have read or are in the process of reading.

DATE 2/10

STRATEGY FOCUS Use Context Clues

TEXT FOR STRATEGY MODELING A Drop of Water by Walter Wick

GROUP MEMBERS Mia, Nora, Oliver, Ben

Before Reading

Mrs. Garza begins the lesson by setting the purpose for reading.

> Readers, I pulled you together today because we need to work more on how we figure out what words mean. We've learned that sometimes the author directly defines vocabulary in the text.

On the board, Mrs. Garza writes the following sentences:

The basketball player's dunk was unprecedented.

This means that no one had done it before.

Before Reading: Mrs. Garza models the strategy.

Here, the author provides a definition of the unfamiliar word, *unprecedented*. It's helpful to us readers when authors provide the meaning of an unfamiliar word. But it's often the case that we encounter new words and have to figure them out without the author's help.

Other times, there are context clues that we can use to find the meaning of the word. Those clues may be in the same sentence or in some sentences before or after. Today we're going to practice the strategy of using context clues to define words so we can understand what we're reading.

Then she provides a model for students.

Let me show you an example of what I mean. We've read this book before. It's called *A Drop of Water* by Walter Wick. When I read page 21, I was unsure of the meaning of the word *rigid*.

SUPPORTING ENGLISH LEARNERS

- When ELs struggle with meaning, it's vital to give them opportunities to verbalize their understanding of their reading and their thinking process. This helps us understand the nature of their challenges. Strategy groups can provide more time for collaborative conversation.
- Extension activities should also include collaborative opportunities with peers to provide students with more talk time.
- Connecting strategy use to listening, speaking, reading, and writing will support transfer of learning.

Listen while I read these sentences, and I will show you how I used clues to understand the meaning of the word *rigid*.

"When water freezes, the molecules lock together forming a rigid structure. A drop of blue water no longer moves. The water has changed from a liquid to a solid—ice."

I already understood the meaning of *structure*. It's something that has been built. But I didn't know the meaning of the word *rigid*. I noticed that the author did not provide a direct definition of the word *rigid*, but he gave me clues. There are two main clues that I used to understand the meaning of *rigid*.
1. The text says that water no longer moves.
2. It also says that the water has changed from a liquid to a solid.

Using these clues, I inferred that *rigid* means something that does not move and is solid.

Let's work together to use clues to find the meaning of another word in another paragraph.

"This snowflake is shown 60 times its actual size. The angles between the six major branches are repeated in many of the smaller details of this amazing structure. How can such an intricate object form in the sky?"

What clues does the author use to help us understand the word *intricate*?

Students suggest that *intricate* means something is complicated and may have many parts.

Today while you read your book, be on the lookout for words you don't know. Then, search for context clues that will help

During Reading: Mrs. Garza confers with a student to help him use context clues to understand vocabulary.

you understand what each word means. Put a self-stick note beside the clues so that you can share your thinking during our discussion.

During Reading

Mrs. Garza gets up and moves around to confer with individual students in the context strategy group. She reminds them of the purpose for today's reading, and asks them to explain their thinking to gather important formative assessment information.

Tell me about the note you've placed in the book. What word puzzled you? What clues did you find? How did you use those clues to help you understand the word?

Before Reading:
Ms. Cary sets the
purpose for reading.

Before Reading

Ms. Cary opens the lesson by reminding students about the book and the purpose of today's lesson.

> When we first read *Horseshoe Soup,* we read it to find out how and why Calamity Jane made horseshoe soup. Today, we're going to reread some pages from this book and think about how the author arranged the events in the story. We will keep track of our thinking on self-stick notes as we reread.

Next, Ms. Cary provides information about story structure.

> When I think about a story, I think about the problem the characters have in the beginning and how that leads to the next events. I think about how the characters finally solve their problem. I use both the words and illustrations to understand the character's problem and their actions. When I am reading closely, I am thinking about the problem in the story and making notes as I read. This is called "annotating the story."

During Reading

Ms. Cary asks students to reread pages 2 and 3. As students read, she listens in, prompting and coaching as needed. She reminds students to make notes as they are reading, and supports students with writing them.

> The problem Calamity Jane has is that she is very hungry. You are reading to find out what she does first to solve her problem. Put a self-stick note with your comments when you read the problem. Then put another note when you find a way she tries to solve her problem.

Students reread several more pages in the text, thinking about what else Calamity Jane does to solve her problem, and making notes as they read.

After Reading:
Ms. Cary engages students in collaborative conversation about the text.

After Reading

Ms. Cary ends the lesson by engaging students in a collaborative conversation.

> We have read about Calamity Jane's problem—that she is hungry—and the events that tell how she tries to solve this problem. Turn and talk with a partner about what Calamity Jane does. Share the notes you made with each other and open the book to reread where you made a note.

Ms. Cary supports students by providing them with the sentence frames:

Next, Calamity Jane _____ and people in town _____.

She ends the lesson by reminding students to think about the problem in the stories they read, and how that problem leads to the next events in the story. She tells them that the notes they take as they read closely help them understand their reading.

Close reading requires that students "dig deeper" into what they read to construct new understandings, develop nuanced meaning, and examine different aspects of text. Close reading should help students move beyond the literal meaning of a text. Related, our assessment should accomplish two goals: First, we must be certain that students establish literal understanding. We can assess this by using main idea questions, asking students to summarize, and through listening to student retellings and discussions of text. Second, we must go beyond the literal understanding to assess close reading—focusing on things like text structure, problem-solving, analysis, and critical evaluation. Ms. Cary did both—and also listened carefully to students' conversations. Finally, she used sentence frames to gauge students' ongoing development as close readers.

I Close Reading Lesson

Mr. Marcus meets with a group of Grade 4 students to do a close reading lesson within guided reading. This is the third time the group will revisit the text, and this time they will explore the text's structure and the author's purpose for using this structure, which has been a focus of whole-group instruction. Mr. Marcus will have students closely read two pages of the text.

DATE 4/6

TEXT FOR STRATEGY MODELING: *After the Earthquake*

STRATEGY FOCUS *Cause-and-Effect Text Structure*

GROUP MEMBERS: *Abigail, Samantha, Renato*

Before Reading

Mr. Marcus opens the lesson by stating the purpose of the lesson.

In our whole-group lessons, we've been exploring the ways authors use text structure to help us understand what we read. We've also been learning about how doing a close reading of a text can help us deepen our understanding of it. Today, we're going to think about text structure as we reread some pages from *After the Earthquake.* We will annotate the text, using self-stick notes to mark places where we notice aspects of the structure.

Mr. Marcus holds up the book.

On page 4, the author asks, "What causes the shaking during an earthquake?" Then he answers the question by explaining that movement of Earth's tectonic plates causes the ground to shake. So the cause is the movement of tectonic plates and the effect is the shaking ground. I will make a note to show my thinking about the text and to record the evidence I found.

Turn to page 6 and reread it. Look for words that tell you what text structure the author used. Annotate the text by placing a note on the page where you find evidence of the text structure.

Before Reading: Mr. Marcus coaches and prompts individual students as needed.

Students reread the page. When all students have finished, they begin to discuss the text. Mr. Marcus observes and takes anecdotal notes about students' understanding and engagement with the text.

During Reading

Then Mr. Marcus has students read the next page on their own.

Now read page 7 and think about cause and effect as you read it.

As he observes, he asks individual students to read aloud quietly as he listens in. He coaches and prompts them as needed. He encourages them to annotate the text as they find evidence.

We're looking more closely at the text to see where the author tells us a cause and an effect. Can you tell what you've found? Look at your annotations to see if you recorded evidence of this.

ways to transfer
learning to
independence

Instead of . . .	Try . . .
Calling on a few raised hands during a discussion	**Asking all students to engage** - Ask students to draw or quick-write their responses first. - Have students turn and talk with a partner before the whole-group discussion.
Conducting a discussion with you doing most of the talking	**Student-led discussions** - Avoid repeating or rephrasing what students say. - Encourage students to elaborate on student responses: "Can anyone build on that?" "Thoughts?"
Reading most of the text to students	**Getting students to read and reread** - Reread this paragraph to yourself. - Partner-read. - Read together.
Deciding what is tricky and directing students to strategies	**Asking students to self-assess and problem-solve** - What made this difficult? - What have you tried? - What could you try?

After Reading

Mr. Marcus wraps up the lesson by asking students to share their thinking.

> How does the cause-and-effect structure help us better understand what we read? How did our annotations help us read closely?

Determining author's purpose is an important close reading strategy. The accomplished students in Mr. Marcus's class were tasked with focusing on different text structures and determining how they contributed to the meaning of text. Students used self-stick notes to mark different text structures, and made annotations related to text structure. Mr. Marcus used the notes and annotations to construct an understanding of each students' close reading related to text structure. In addition, he listened as students read and explained their strategies. He asked questions that linked students' work with text structure to their comprehension of the text.

Concluding Thoughts

Close reading instruction begins during whole-group lessons, but students can apply and develop this skill very quickly while working in small groups. To accomplish this, model what close reading looks like—using annotation, highlighting, rereading, and collaborating. Close reading can also be a follow-up strategy during strategy group or guided reading group instruction. This will help students develop the habit of returning to the text to delve deeper into the "well of deep understanding."

Reflecting on Your Teaching

Here are some questions to help you reflect on your teaching and to guide professional learning discussions:

- How can you provide strong models of close reading for your students?
- How do you encourage collaborative conversations during close reading lessons?
- How would close reading and annotations look in your classroom?
- How would you use annotations to identify students' needs?

FURTHER READING

Unlocking Close Reading by Linda Feaman and Nancy Geldermann (Maupin House, 2015).

Text-Dependent Questions Grades K–5: Pathways to Close and Critical Reading by Douglas Fisher and Nancy Frey (Corwin Press, 2014).

Rigorous Reading by Nancy Frey and Douglas Fisher (Corwin Press, 2013).

"The Compelling Why: Using Short Texts to Support Close Reading" by Adria F. Klein *http://edublog.scholastic.com/post/compelling-why-using-short-texts-support-close-reading* (June 30, 2016).

A Close Look at Close Reading: Teaching Students to Analyze Complex Texts, Grades K–5 by Dianne Lapp and Barbara Moss (Association for Supervision and Curriculum, 2015).

Falling in Love with Close Reading by Christopher Lehman and Kathleen Roberts (Heinemann, 2013).

Teaching Reading in Small Groups by Jennifer Serravallo (Heinemann, 2010).

CHAPTER 4

LITERACY WORK TIME

"The most common question I get from teachers who are new to guided reading is 'What are the other children doing while I'm teaching a small group?' My answer is always 'Keep it simple. They should be reading, writing, listening, and speaking (softly).'"

Jan Richardson, 2016

E ach day, students spend more time working independently than they do meeting with us in small groups. We need to ensure that this time is put to productive use. Planning effective literacy activities that connect to the work we are doing in whole-group and small-group lessons, and having routines in place that support students' independence are essential. Effective independent work time also supports teaching for transfer by providing another context in which students can practice and apply their learning. During this time, you may be working with a small group, but you might spend some time conferring with students, helping them set and achieve personal learning goals.

TOPICS IN THIS CHAPTER

Organizing and managing your classroom

•

Establishing routines

•

Determining the focus of literacy work time activities

•

Planning effective literacy activities

•

Conferring with students

It is important that classroom organization both give students places to collaborate and to work independently.

What You Need to Know About Literacy Work Time

Every classroom should be a community of learners in which students take responsibility for their own learning, and work together to problem-solve questions and issues. For this type of classroom community to develop, it's important to create an organized environment where students respect and support one another. Clearly defined expectations and fully understood routines contribute to positive learning outcomes during independent work time. Giving students choices about the activities they participate in is also key to making the learning outcomes effective. Then, as we confer with individual students, we can gather formative assessment data to help us plan for learning opportunities in the classroom community.

Organizing and Managing Your Classroom to Build Community and Support Independence

Situate your small-group teaching area so that you can observe students as they work independently. Once you've decided on the types of student learning activities, decide what materials are needed for these areas and how you want to store the materials when they are not in use. Some teachers share photographs of how students should work together and how the work area should look when students are finished working there. How you set up and manage independent work areas will vary depending on the grade level of students and their experience with this type of classroom.

Students can move from area to area individually or in small groups. Avoid keeping students in the same group they were in for small-group reading. It is too easy to assume that students who work together in a small group should also work together during literacy work time. However, there are benefits to having students work in heterogeneous groups in this part of the literacy block.

Giving students some choice in the activities they participate in will increase motivation and engagement. Some teachers use self-paced weekly contracts that list several options for students to choose during literacy work time. You can make some selections for students to ensure that they are receiving the practice they need—but allow them to make some of their own choices. A place for listing personal goals is also part of this contract.

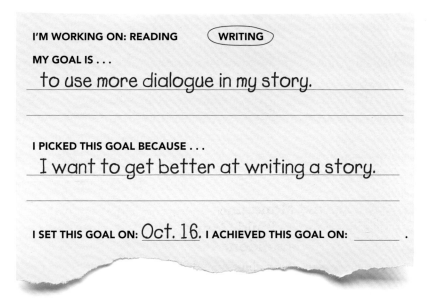

I'M WORKING ON: READING   (WRITING)

MY GOAL IS . . .
to use more dialogue in my story.

I PICKED THIS GOAL BECAUSE . . .
I want to get better at writing a story.

I SET THIS GOAL ON: Oct. 16. I ACHIEVED THIS GOAL ON: _____ .

Establishing Routines

As literacy educator Kathy Collins said, "When we follow routines day after day, our students can use their energy to grow as readers and learners rather than to figure out what we expect them to do. And we, in turn, can focus our energy on teaching, not managing, our independent learners." Investing time at the beginning of the year to teach routines will ensure that students have a true understanding of appropriate ways to work independently as well as our expectations for their work. Effective routines will help students stay on task and be responsible for their own learning, and will provide them with consistency that supports the transfer of learning.

Effective Modeling

An effective way to model a routine is to have students watch you perform the routine and then tell you in their own words the behaviors they see. This makes the routine more concrete and specific for students. After you have modeled each step, you can create a

Literacy Work Time Essentials

- Locate your small-group instruction area so that while you teach you have a view of all students who are working independently.
- Take advantage of the space that you have designed to observe and listen to your students.
- The classroom library should be the focal point of your classroom. It should be accessible and easily managed by students.
- Work areas should be configured appropriately so they can accommodate students who will work with partners or in small groups.
- Create and display anchor charts that help students understand expectations and routines for each work area. Ideally, these charts should be created interactively by teachers and students during the early part of the school year, so that routines are established quickly and students know they are expected to follow them.
- Ensure that students are confident about the use of all materials and know how and where they can access them.
- Be clear about how and when you will consult with other students and groups. Students need to know when they can ask for teacher support.

a small group of students reading books independently

chart that outlines the expected behaviors. You can use such charts to redirect students who are off task. Here are some tactics to keep in mind as you support students in describing your actions.

• Think through and practice the specific behaviors that you want to demonstrate (e.g., speak quietly, use eye contact) to keep the presentation focused and to elicit all the types of behaviors you want.

• Make sure students always focus on the positive. (For example, have them say, "You spoke in a quiet voice," not "You didn't yell.") This keeps the focus on the behavior you want students to adopt.

• Keep your chart short and specific. State each behavior simply so that students can easily remember it. If the list gets long, you may want to simplify the task or break it into steps and model each one. Be sure the print on the chart is large enough for it to be seen at a distance.

• Regularly refer to the chart to help students get in the habit of doing so themselves.

Below is an example of this type of modeling. Note that the teacher slightly exaggerates the underlined language and behaviors to emphasize the specific language students might use.

> **Teacher:** Today I want to show you how to partner-read. I'm going to model the rules with Cara. Cara and I will take turns reading one page, telling each other what we learned, and then asking a question about what will happen next. Everyone, watch us. What behaviors do you notice?

The teacher reads, stumbles on the word *rough* and stops.

> **Teacher:** (*looking at partner*) Can you help me with this word?
> **Cara:** Sure. It's *rough.*
> **Teacher:** *Rough.* Thank you. I think *rough* water means that there were a lot of waves. That's what I see in the picture. What do you think?
> **Cara:** I agree.

The teacher reads to the end of the page and stops.

> **Teacher:** *(looking at Cara)* On this page I learned that a woman fell into the ocean and no one saw her. She was swimming and then she felt something bump her. <u>Do you want to add anything?</u>
>
> **Cara:** *(shakes her head)* What do you think will happen next?
>
> **Teacher:** I think she's going to see a dolphin because that's the title of the book! Okay, your turn.
>
> **Cara:** *(reads the next page)* On this page, I learned that the woman sees something and she thinks it's a shark but it's a dolphin. *(pauses)*
>
> **Teacher:** *(making eye contact with Cara)* <u>Are you done? Can I add something?</u> *(Cara nods)*
>
> **Teacher:** The dolphin saves her life. <u>What do you think will happen next?</u> *(stops the modeling and looks at the class)*
>
> **Teacher:** What did you notice about how Cara and I did partner-reading?
>
> **Students:** You looked at Cara when you talked. You said "thank you" when Cara helped you. You asked Cara if she was done and if you could add something.

By watching and articulating the specific actions of the teacher and student, students cement their understanding of the routine.

Literacy Activities That Support Independence

The purpose of literacy work time is to provide students with opportunities to practice and apply strategies that have already been modeled and taught during whole-group instruction and then practiced during small-group instruction. Consider the following as you choose activities for students.

- Students should be productively engaged in literacy learning.
- Students should practice and apply strategies and concepts that have already been taught. They should apply these strategies to texts that can be read easily.
- Students should use listening, speaking, reading, and writing as vehicles to demonstrate learning.

Literacy Routines and Activities:

The table suggests a variety of routines and activities to implement during literacy work time. The goal is for students to read, write, listen, and talk. You may want to organize your classroom with three or four activities. Remember to model these routines first before expecting students to implement.

ACTIVITY	DESCRIPTION
Independent Reading	All students should spend some time each day reading independently. Giving students both time to read and a choice in what they read is one of the most powerful ways to support their reading growth and increase their stamina.
Partner-Reading	Partner-reading gives students an opportunity to model fluency for each other and to practice cooperative skills, such as taking turns.
Writing	Writing activities are an important part of a comprehensive literacy classroom. Students can write in response to what they've read during small groups or during independent reading. Writing center activities might include constructed response, free writing, and writing to sources.
Listening	At this center, provide books and a device for students to hear the audio. Ideally, students should listen on headphones to keep the noise level in the classroom down.
Book Clubs (or Novel Studies Groups or Literature Circles)	Many teachers begin book clubs in small group, using that time to help students choose a book, determine a reading schedule, and establish routines. But once students understand the routines, they can meet to discuss the book during independent work time, with the teacher periodically joining their conversations. Some teachers ask students to take on specific roles (such as director or summarizer), but the main goal is for groups to understand how to have productive, collaborative conversations.
Reader's Theater (Grade 1 and Up)	Reader's theater is a motivating way to have a group of students reread texts. Students don't need to memorize their part. Instead, they hold their scripts and use facial expressions, gestures, and different voice tones as they perform. Reader's theater gives students an authentic reason to reread a text. Establish an area of the classroom where students can practice reading together.
Technology	E-books provide options that allow you to scaffold students. Many e-books include pronunciation guides and definitions. Some e-book apps allow you to turn the narration on and off. A student can listen with the narration on at first and then try reading with it off.
Conferring	As students read independently, have quick, focused conversations. Note your observations and have students record their next goals on a contract or in a reading notebook.

ROUTINES	ASSESSMENT
• Use the library. • Self-select texts. • Choose a place to read. • Orally rehearse a response before writing. • Be prepared by bringing a response journal and pencil to the workstation. • Follow protocols for collaborative conversation.	• Observe and listen to your students. • Check on students' ability to use library and media center resources. • Determine that your students have the ability to choose appropriate reading materials. • Ask questions that help you understand the students' comprehension of independently read texts. • Keep track of students' motivation and engagement. • Examine students' independent reading logs. • Consider projects to complement students' independent reading.
• Use appropriate voice volume. • Choose a book. • Take turns while reading. • Help your partner. • Ask questions.	• Use a measure of oral reading fluency to check on student development. • Develop and use a checklist that focuses on students' cooperative skills, including turn taking and providing valuable feedback.
• Use a response journal. • Use the materials in the center. • Give classmates helpful feedback on their writing.	• Examine students' response journals. • Determine students' ability to use and follow a writing rubric. • Observe students' conversations as they provide one another with feedback on writing.
• Take turns turning the audio device off and on. • Respond to the book.	• Ask questions that focus on students' listening comprehension. • Evaluate students' retellings of stories.
• Follow protocols for collaborative conversation. • Determine a reading schedule. • Note points in the book to talk about.	• Ask questions that focus on students' listening comprehension. • Evaluate students' retellings of stories.
• Speak at an appropriate volume. • Speak with appropriate emphasis and tone. • Support other readers in the group.	• Use a checklist to evaluate students' collaborative conversations. • Ask questions about students' participation in book club. • Determine students' adherence to the particular book club routines.
• Use the device. • Learn how to start and how to stop.	• Use a checklist to determine students' familiarity with and mastery of reading and technology.
• Share progress toward a goal.	• Use a metacognitive checklist with students to help them focus on goals, and to note their progress toward goals. • In conversation, evaluate students' progress and provide feedback.

students engaged in a workstation during independent learning

Independent Reading and Conferring

We cannot stress enough the importance of independent reading. It is an essential literacy activity and one that students should participate in every day, with students having a choice in what they read. As literacy researchers Dick Allington and Rachael Gabriel (2012) have stated, "The research base on student-selected reading is robust and conclusive. Students read more, understand more, and are more likely to continue reading when they have the opportunity to choose what they read."

Conferring is also part of an effective literacy program. Conferring is the time to check in on independent reading, help students set personal goals, and listen to them reread a short section of a book they are currently reading. You might also use this time to take an informational oral reading record (see pages 16–17) or to prompt students during the reading to help nudge them to use strategies they know. This isn't a time to test students; it is a time to observe and scaffold specifically for what each student is learning. With strong organization and planning, it's possible to spend three to five minutes with each student once within a two- to three-week period. There are often opportunities to do this between meeting with small groups.

In Action

Let's take a look at how literacy work time happens in two classrooms. The teachers in both classrooms have established routines so that students can work independently.

P Literacy Work Time

Mr. Philips, a Grade 1 teacher, is about to begin his first guided reading lesson of the morning.

He settles in with a group of six students. The other students check the choice board and move to one of the five literacy centers in the classroom. Mr. Philips had introduced each center at the beginning of the year and carefully modeled the routines for each one several times. Charts placed strategically throughout the classroom remind students of important center routines, such as how to have a collaborative conversation, self-select a book, and orally rehearse a response before writing.

Eddie, Jason, Molly, and Yoko move to the reading nook. Each selects a book to read from the classroom library and finds a place to read. Olivia and Jayden have chosen to listen to audiobooks in the listening center.

Lila, Axel, Jorge, and Shawn find their response journals and sit down to work in the writing center. Jorge asks Shawn to listen to him as he rehearses the story he plans to write. He talks quietly, and Shawn responds by making a few suggestions. After this rehearsal, Jorge begins to write and Shawn returns to his own writing.

Two students, Mark and Mandy, have chosen to do partner-reading. They briefly discuss and choose the three titles they will read. They sit side by side, sharing the book. They decide that Mark will read first. They read their book, taking turns. When they finish, they talk about their favorite part of the book. Finally, Mark and Mandy draw a picture in their journal that tells about that part.

Our Jobs during Reading Workstation
Be a partner.
Be a listener.
Be a speaker.
Be a reader.

Library Workstation
Handle books carefully.
Put books away where they belong.
Read quietly.

Anchor charts help students understand expectations and routines for workstations.

I Literacy Work Time

In Mrs. Clark's Grade 5 classroom, some students are reading independently, others are working at a workstation, completing a book summary graphic organizer—summarizing was a recent focus of whole-group and small-group instruction. Another group of four students is doing reader's theater.

As Mrs. Clark scans the classroom, she notices that Jenna, one of the students in the independent reading area, is off task. To help Jenna get back on track, she reminds her to review the chart that explains what to do during independent reading. The review chart provides structure and guidance for Jenna.

The students in the group doing reader's theater have scripts and they have chosen parts. Today, they are reading the scripts from beginning to end to practice phrasing and intonation.

The group reads through the script, trying out different ways to read some of the lines. They support one another, making suggestions about what words to emphasize. Mrs. Clark has modeled using an appropriate voice level, so students know how to practice without being disruptive. When it's time to move to the next rotation, the students store their scripts and move to their next activity.

Active Listener
- Have eyes on the speaker.
- Maintain a quiet body.
- Use appropriate expressions to show interest.
- Be patient while the speaker chooses what to say. Give enough wait time.
- Think carefully about what the speaker is saying.

Use anchor charts to encourage active listening.

Concluding Thoughts

Literacy work time is an important part of small-group reading. If organized effectively, it allows you to work with a small group, knowing that other students are engaged in productive literacy work. This time is also important because it puts students in charge of their own learning. Students have opportunities to make decisions for themselves, helping them become independent learners. In an effective comprehensive literacy classroom, providing time for independent work is a gift for our students, giving them valuable time to build their love of reading and maximize their learning.

Reflecting on Your Teaching

Here are some questions to help you reflect on your teaching and to guide professional learning discussions:

• What are some ways you coordinate the activities students do during independent work with your whole-group and small-group lessons?

• What is one thing you could do tomorrow to improve your students' understanding of your expectations during literacy work time?

• What strategy do you find most effective in keeping students on task?

• How can conferring and formative assessment help you personalize the learning in the classroom community?

FURTHER READING

"E-Books and E-Book Apps: Considerations for Beginning Readers" by C. C. Bates, Adria F. Klein, B. Schubert, A. McGee, N. Anderson, L. Dorn, E. McClure, and R. H. Ross in *The Reading Teacher*, January/February 2017.

The Daily Five by Gail Boushey and Joan Moser (Stenhouse, 2006).

The Café Book by Gail Boushey and Joan Moser (Stenhouse, 2009).

Growing Readers: Units of Study in the Primary Classroom by Kathy Collins (Stenhouse, 2004).

I Am Reading: Nurturing Young Children's Meaning Making and Joyful Engagement with Any Book by Kathy Collins and Matt Glover (Heinemann, 2015).

Classrooms That Work: They Can All Read and Write by Patricia Cunningham and Richard Allington (Pearson, 2015).

Comprehension from the Ground Up by Sharon Taberski (Heinemann, 2010).

Partner-reading is a good strategy to improve fluency and vocabulary, as students will work together to build vocabulary and content knowledge.

References

Afflerbach, P., Pearson, P. & Paris, S. G. (2008). Clarifying differences between reading skills and reading strategies. *The Reading Teacher, 61* (5), 364–373.

Allington, R., & Gabriel, R. (2012). Every child, every day. *Educational Leadership, 69* (6), 10–15.

Bates, C. C., Klein, A., Schubert, B., McGee, A., Anderson, N., Dorn, L., McClure, E., & Ross, R. H. (2017). E-books and e-book apps: Considerations for beginning readers. *The Reading Teacher, 70* (4), 401–411.

Bormouth, J. R. (1975). Literacy in the classroom. In W. D. Page (Ed.) *Help for the reading teacher: New directions in research*, 60–90. Urbana, IL: National Conference on Research in English and ERIC/RCS Clearinghouse.

Bruner, J. (1986). *Actual minds, possible words.* Cambridge, MA: Harvard University.

Calkins, L. (2015). *A guide to reading workshop.* Portsmouth, NH: Heinemann.

Collins, K. (2004). *Growing readers: Units of study in the primary classroom.* Portland, ME: Stenhouse.

Collins, K. & Glover, M. (2015). *I am reading: Nurturing young children's meaning making and joyful engagement with any book.* Portsmouth, NH: Heinemann.

DeFord, D., & Klein, A. (2008). Teacher decision making is the key to choosing among leveled books and going beyond. In K. Szymusiak, F. Sibberson, & L. Portland Koch (Eds.) *Beyond leveled books: Supporting early and transitional readers in grades K–5* (2nd Ed.), 7–16. Portland, ME: Stenhouse.

Duke, N. K., & Pearson, P. D. (2002). Effective practices for developing reading comprehension. In A. E. Farstrup, & S. J. Samuels (Eds.) *What research has to say about reading instruction,* 205–242. Newark, DE: International Reading Association.

Fisher, D., & Frey, N. (2012). Close reading in elementary schools. *The Reading Teacher, 66,* 179–188.

Flesch, R. (1948) A new readability yardstick. *Journal of Applied Psychology*, 32 (3), 221–233.

Ford, M. P., & Opitz, M. F. (2011). Looking back to move forward with guided reading. *Reading Horizons,* 50 (4), 225–240.

Fountas, I., & Pinnell, G. S. (2016). *The Fountas and Pinnell literacy continuum* (Expanded Ed.). Portsmouth, NH: Heinemann.

Fountas, I. C. & Pinnell, G. S. (1996). *Guided reading: Good first teaching for all children.* Portsmouth, NH: Heinemann.

Fry, E. (1968). A readability formula that saves time. *Journal of Reading* 11 (7), 513–516, 575–578.

Klein, A. F. (2016, June 30). The compelling why: Using short texts to support close reading. Retrieved from http://edublog.scholastic.com/post/compelling-why-using-short-texts-support-close-reading.

Paris, S., Lipson, M. & Wixson, K. (1983). Becoming a strategic reader. *Contemporary Educational Psychology*, 8 (1), 293–316.

Pearson, P. D., & Gallagher, M. C. (1983). The instruction of reading comprehension. *Contemporary Educational Psychology,* 8, 317–344.

Pressley, M. & Afflerbach, P. (1995). *Verbal protocols of reading: The nature of constructively responsive reading.* New York, NY: Routledge.

Richardson, J. (2016). *The next step forward in guided reading.* New York, NY: Scholastic.

Routman, R. (2002). *Reading essentials.* Portsmouth, NH: Heinemann.

Serravallo, J. (2010). *Teaching reading in small groups.* Portsmouth, NH: Heinemann.

Swartz, S. L., Shook, R. E., Klein, A. F. et al. (2003). *Guided reading and literacy centers.* San Diego, CA: Dominie Press, Inc.

Thorndike, E. L. (1921/2009). *The teacher's word book.* Ithaca, NY: Cornell University Library.

Glossary

balanced literacy. A model for learning instruction in elementary grades that includes both reading and writing instruction in a variety of classroom settings. The model incorporates or includes three workshop components: reading workshop, writing workshop, and word work.

close reading. An instructional strategy that involves detailed analysis and annotation of a text, often occurring through repeated exposures.

closing. (See also *mini-lesson*.) The portion of a lesson during which a teacher summarizes and concludes instruction, often done in a whole-group setting.

cognates. Words that are spelled or pronounced the same or similarly, e.g., *hora* in Spanish, which corresponds to *hour* in English.

collaborative conversation. Dialogue involving several participants that is shared through multiple exchanges.

complex texts. (See *text complexity*.)

comprehension. The ability to derive meaning from print and understand text. At a literal level, comprehension involves understanding what an author explicitly says or illustrates through details provided in a text. At a higher-order level, comprehension involves reflective and purposeful understanding and inference.

comprehensive literacy. An approach to reading and writing instruction across content areas that emphasizes five components: phonemic awareness, phonics, fluency, vocabulary, and text comprehension.

conferring. Teacher-initiated conversations with individual students that aim to facilitate students' reflection on their thinking, reading, and writing processes.

cross-linguistic transfer. Applying first-language skills and knowledge to comparable domains in a second language.

developmental reading levels. A continuum that explains how students progress as readers.

emergent: Designates a stage of reading development in which students have a basic understanding of the alphabet, phonological awareness, early phonics, and a significant number of high-frequency words. Emergent readers recognize different types of text, both fiction and nonfiction, and are learning to apply comprehension strategies and word-attack skills.

emergent/early: A beginning stage of reading development in which aspiring readers are learning basic print concepts, uppercase and lowercase letters, and a variety of phonological skills, including how to recognize phonemes, syllables, and rhyme. Instruction for emergent/early readers focuses on sound/symbol relationships, beginning with consonants and short vowels; therefore, these students may read CVC (consonant-vowel-consonant) words and some high-frequency words.

early/fluent: Another stage of reading development in which reading processes become more automatic so that students can focus their attention more on comprehension than on word attack and decoding. Students begin to read more independently and to understand differences in style and genre while reading a greater variety of texts.

fluent: A final stage of reading development in which students move away from the concept of "learning to read" and toward that of "reading to learn." Students read more automatically with enhanced prosody (expression and proper pauses), focusing on comprehension through the application of various comprehension strategies.

Glossary

primary. **P** Students in Kindergarten through Grade 2.

print concepts. Basic concepts about print that include identification of a book's front and back covers and title page; directionality (in English, reading from left to right, top to bottom, front to back); spacing (distance used to separate words); recognition of letters and words; sound/symbol relationships; capitalization and punctuation; and sequencing and locating skills.

prosody. The defining feature of expressive reading that combines all the variables of timing, phrasing, emphasis, and intonation used to make reading lively and comprehensible.

reading skill. A student's developmental level of automaticity that involves decoding and comprehending texts with speed, efficiency, and fluency.

reading strategy. A deliberate, goal-directed approach that readers adopt in order to control or modify their efforts to decode text, understand words, and construct meanings from text.

Response to Intervention (RtI, RtI²). A multi-level instructional/assessment response system designed to support student achievement and prevent or reduce behavior disruptions. Often called response to intervention (RtI), or response to intervention and instruction (RtI²).

running record. (See also *oral reading record*.) A tool that helps teachers identify patterns in student reading behaviors and/or an instructional reading level for individual students (when paired with comprehension inquiry).

scaffolding. Temporary assistance provided to a student by a teacher, another adult, or a more capable peer, enabling the student to perform a task the student otherwise would not be able to complete alone, with the goal of fostering the student's capacity to perform the task alone eventually.